DISASTERS

DISASTERS

The Biggest Disasters in History
From Salt in the Indus Valley to Hurricane Sandy

KIERON CONNOLLY

SCHOLASTIC

www.scholastic.com

This edition published by Scholastic Inc., 557 Broadway, New York, NY 10012 by arrangement with Amber Books Ltd.

Scholastic Canada Ltd.
Markham, Ontario

Scholastic Australia Pty. Ltd
Gosford NSW

Scholastic New Zealand Ltd.
Greenmount, Auckland

1 2 3 4 5 6 7 8 9 10

ISBN: 978-0-545-55565-4

Editorial and design by
Amber Books Ltd
74–77 White Lion Street
London N1 9PF
United Kingdom
www.amberbooks.co.uk

Project Editor: Sarah Uttridge
Design: Colin Fielder
Picture Research: Terry Forshaw

Printed in Shenzhen, China

Picture credits:
Alamy: 9 (Anders Blomqvist), 10 (Realy Easy Star/Tulliop Valente), 17 (PAC), 18 (Interfoto), 27 (North Wind), 32 (Art Archive), 36 (North Wind), 42 (North Wind), 49 (Terry Whittaker), 65 (Interfoto), 78-79 (Accent Alaska), 80 (Michael Patrick O'Neill), 81 (Zuma), 83 (Dinodia Photos), 86 (Alamy Celebrity), 87 (Aurora Photos/Natalie Behring), 94 (Richard Levine)
Corbis: 8 (David Samuel Robbins), 12 (Peter Philipp/Harald Jahn), 15 (Roger Ressmeyer), 19 (Heritage Images), 22, 28 (Heritage Images), 30 (Reuters/Lisbon City Museum), 33 (Lebrecht Music & Arts), 37 (National Geographical Society/Jim Richardson), 38 (Robert Harding World imagery/Tuul), 41 (Bettmann), 43, 46 (Ralph White), 47 (National Geographical Society), 52 (Bettmann), 60-62 all (Bettmann), 67 (David Turnley), 68 (Bettmann), 71 (Steve Terrill), 72 (Sygma/Kapoor Balder), 73 (Bettmann), 74 (Peter Turnley), 75 (Sygma/Thierry Orban), 76 (Reuters), 82 (Reuters/ Lana Silvar), 90 (David Guttenfelder), 91 (Zuma/Issei Kato-Pool), 93 bottom left (Andrew Lichtenstein), 93 right (Star Ledger/Aristide Economopoulus), 95 bottom left (Steven Greaves), 95 top right (EPA/Jean Jacques Augustin), 95 bottom right (Star Ledger/David Gard)
Nik Cornish/Stavka.org.uk: 56
Dorling Kindersley: 25
Dreamstime: 16 (Luciano Mortula), 20 (Galina Barskaya), 48 (Bgillard), 88 (Arindam Banerjee), 89 (Concetta Zingale)
Mary Evans Picture Library: 13, 23, 31, 39 (ILN), 54 (ILN), 55 (ILN)
FEMA: 82
FLPA: 21 (Imagebroker/Angela Speer)
Getty: 11 (National Geographic), 14 (Gamma-Rapho/Marc Deville), 24 (Bridgeman/James Edwin McConnell), 26 (Archive Photos), 29 (Hulton), 34 (Bloomberg/Adam Majendie), 63 (Hulton), 69 (Popperfoto), 77 (National Geographic/Steven L. Rayner), 93 top left (AFP/Jewel Samad), 95 top left (Boston Globe)
Library of Congress: 7, 40, 44, 45, 58, 59, 64
NASA: 35, 66, 84
Photoshot: 83 (WPN)
Public Domain: 50, 51
Topfoto: 53, 57
U.S. Department of Defense: 85, 92
U.S. Geological Survey: 6, 70

Contents

BCE = Before the Common Era
CE = Common Era

INTRODUCTION

A disaster can last less than a minute, but its effect can be felt for decades. A disaster can be as enormous as a volcano, as small as a rat, or even invisible to the naked eye, such as bacteria. Some disasters cause a great loss of human life; others affect wildlife and the environment.

From the ancient world to Hurricane Sandy in 2012, this book looks at 43 different disasters. Some are geological disasters—such as earthquakes, volcanoes, and tsunamis; others are caused by the weather, such as hurricanes, tornadoes, and floods; others are caused by bacteria, and others are manmade disasters such as chemical spills, famines, pollution, and accidents.

Surprise hazards

Today, we can detect when a disaster might happen, we can warn each other and move quickly in cars, and we have better medicines. But we also have the technology to create new disasters.

Yet despite all of these disasters, the human race is strong. We may have suffered many disasters, but we've also survived.

American Disasters
Above: After the earthquake in 1906, people in San Francisco watch the city on fire.
Left: The eruption of Mount St. Helens, 1980.

SALT IN THE INDUS VALLEY

WHEN: 1750 BCE

We might not think of salt as something that could cause disasters, but using salty river water on crops destroyed an entire civilization.

Between 3000 and 1500 BCE, one of the earliest and most sophisticated civilizations existed in the Indus Valley. The civilization contained two cities: Harappa and Mohenjo-Daro. These cities had rows of houses and streets, drainage systems and markets like modern cities. But by 1500 BCE, the civilization had collapsed.

Historians believe that as the population of the cities increased, more fields had to be farmed. Farmers watered their crops from the Indus River. However, the salt in the Indus River slowly poisoned the soil. Instead of growing more crops, the civilization produced fewer.

Moving Away

When there wasn't enough food to buy in the cities' markets, the people began to move away to farm new land. The cities fell into ruin.

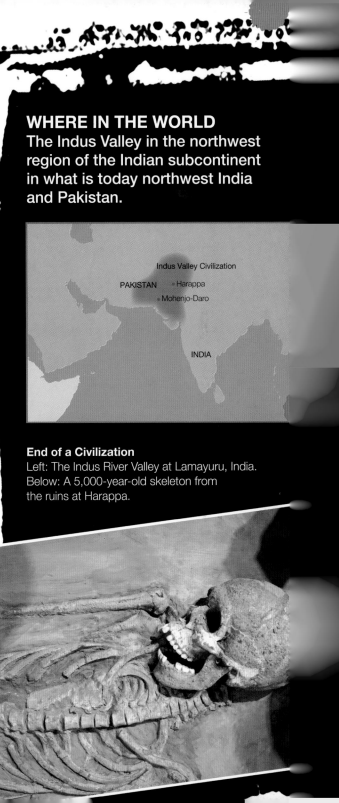

WHERE IN THE WORLD
The Indus Valley in the northwest region of the Indian subcontinent in what is today northwest India and Pakistan.

Indus Valley Civilization
PAKISTAN • Harappa
• Mohenjo-Daro
INDIA

End of a Civilization
Left: The Indus River Valley at Lamayuru, India.
Below: A 5,000-year-old skeleton from the ruins at Harappa.

FACTS

• Our earliest record of a plowed field is in the Harappan region.

• Cities can only exist if farmers can produce enough food for everyone.

• When the Romans defeated Carthage in North Africa in 146 BCE, they spread salt over the land to deliberately spoil it for farming.

• Barley and wheat were the main crops farmed in the Indus Valley.

ERUPTION OF THERA VOLCANO

WHEN: c. 1628 BCE

When the volcano on the island of Thera erupted, it destroyed the island, leaving a massive crater that was filled by the sea.

By the 17th century BCE, Thera was an important part of the Greek world, mainly because of its port, Akrotiri. This was a sophisticated town with paved streets, decorations on the houses, and buildings that had been strengthened with wood supports to protect against volcanic activity and earthquakes.

However, in 1628 BCE, earth tremors made the people desert their homes. As no human remains or precious goods have been found in the ruins at Akrotiri, it's thought that all of the people managed to escape before the volcano erupted.

Ash Cloud

Akrotiri was caught in the blast from the volcano and was completely destroyed. Fortunately for archaeologists, the ash from the volcano preserved the ruins of the town.

WHERE IN THE WORLD
Thera, today called Santorini, is about 70 mi. (110 km) north of the island of Crete in the Mediterranean Sea.

EUROPE

GREECE

• Santorini

Crete

Blasted into the Sky
Right: The people of Akrotiri escape as the volcano erupts. Below: Ruins of a settlement at Thera today.

FACTS

• The powerful volcano ejected an estimated 7.5 cubic mi. (31 cubic km) of ash into the air.

• The volcano left only a crater. The sea water rushed in, creating a tsunami (a giant wave).

• The volcano turned the sky yellow as far away as China.

• Some people believe that the Theran eruption is the origin of the legend of Atlantis, the island civilization that sank to the bottom of the sea.

AEGEAN SEA TSUNAMI

WHEN:
c. 1628 BCE

The Thera volcano set off a tsunami and ash cloud that may have caused the decline of the Minoan civilization on the island of Crete.

The Thera volcano blew itself and much of the island to pieces, leaving a massive crater. This was filled with water and caused a 492 ft. (150 m)-high tsunami moving at 100 mph (160 km/h). The island of Crete was only 70 mi. (110 km) away to the south.

The Minoan civilization on Crete was one of the most sophisticated of its time. It had palaces, large ports, and was an important part of Greek politics. When the tsunami hit, it smashed through the ports on Crete's northern coast, destroying the shipping fleet and damaging palaces. Inland, a cloud of ash and pumice (light volcanic rock) choked the crops.

Volcanic Devastation

The Minoan civilization began to decline around this time, and archaeologists believe that this was because of the devastating effects of the Thera volcano.

WHERE IN THE WORLD
Crete is an island in the Mediterranean Sea about 100 mi. (160 km) south of mainland Greece.

EUROPE

GREECE

• Crete

Minoan Ruins
`Left: The ruins of the palace at Knossos, Crete. Some of the ancient buildings have been rebuilt by archaeologists. Below: The tsunami pounds the coastline settlements.

FACTS

• The wall of water from Thera would have taken only minutes to reach the Cretan coastline.

• Ash clouds from volcanoes blot out the sun, causing a drop in temperature and reducing plant growth.

• The capital of the Minoan civilization was Knossos on Crete.

• According to mythology, in the labyrinth at Knossos lived the Minotaur, a beast that had the head of a bull and the body of a man.

THE DESTRUCTION OF POMPEII

October 24, 79 CE

The city of Pompeii was buried under 20 ft. (6 m) of ash and volcanic rock when Mount Vesuvius erupted.

By 79 CE, Pompeii was a city of about 20,000 people. There had been earthquakes, but the eruption which began on October 24 lasted for two days. At first, ash shot out of the volcano, reaching high into the sky. At this stage, people were still able to escape from the town, but later, hot gas and rock began streaming down from the volcano, destroying buildings and people.

At the height of the eruption, 1.5 million tons of molten rock and pumice were blasted out of the volcano every second. It is estimated that 16,000 people died in the eruption.

Lost in Time

The town was abandoned and forgotten about for more than 1,500 years. In 1599, the ruins were first discovered, but excavations did not begin until 1748.

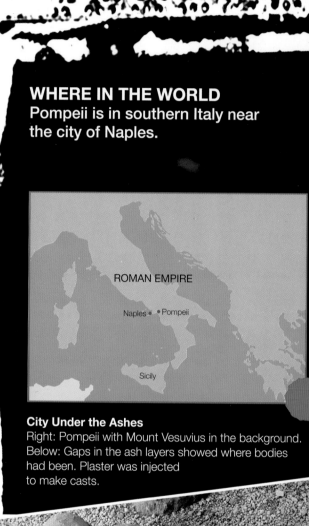

WHERE IN THE WORLD
Pompeii is in southern Italy near the city of Naples.

ROMAN EMPIRE

Naples • • Pompeii

Sicily

City Under the Ashes
Right: Pompeii with Mount Vesuvius in the background.
Below: Gaps in the ash layers showed where bodies had been. Plaster was injected to make casts.

FACTS

• People live near volcanoes because the soil around volcanoes is very fertile and good for farming.

• The eruption happened one day after Vulcanalia, the festival of the Roman god of fire and volcanoes.

• Before the eruption, the town of Pompeii was a popular holiday destination for Romans. Today, people visit Pompeii to see the ruins of the ancient city.

• The ash from the volcano preserved the victims' bodies and the buildings.

COLLAPSE AT THE CIRCUS MAXIMUS

WHEN: 284–300 CE

The Circus Maximus was the great sports stadium in ancient Rome and the site of the biggest sporting disaster in history.

The Circus Maximus was the first and largest Roman circus and had been in use since the 4th century BCE.

With a 1,970-ft. (600-m) track, it was the place to see chariot races. Originally it was built of wood, but as sections were destroyed, they were replaced with stone.

But the Emperor Trajan (98–117 CE) wanted even more people to be able to see him when he attended the races. So he had the wooden upper tier of the stadium rebuilt in stone, which provided seating for 150,000 people.

Falling Rubble

In 140 CE. a pillar in the upper tier gave way, causing the stands to collapse and killing 1,112 spectators. The stadium was rebuilt again, but even worse was to come. In the late 3rd century, a long wall in the upper tier collapsed, killing 13,000 people.

WHERE IN THE WORLD
The ruins of the Circus Maximus can still be seen today in Rome, Italy.

ROMAN EMPIRE

ITALY

Rome

GREECE

End of an Era
Left: Ruins of part of the Imperial Palace on the Palatine Hill overlooking the Circus Maximus. Below: Chariots were pulled by two to four horses.

FACTS

• Circus Maximus means "great circle" in Latin. A Roman circus was a place for big public events.

• Usually horses pulled the chariots, but occasionally, ostriches, dogs, or camels were used.

• The laps were marked by seven models of giant eggs and dolphins. Each time a charioteer completed a lap, one of the models was lowered.

• The last race was held in 549 CE. After this, the Circus Maximus fell into ruin.

LITTLE ICE AGE, NORTHERN HEMISPHERE

c. 1350 –c. 1850

Earthquakes and volcanoes affect people immediately, while disasters such as the little ice age act more gradually but can last for centuries.

Between the 13th century and the 19th century, the temperature in the Northern Hemisphere (north of the equator) dropped. The coldest centuries were between 1550 and 1850.

Climate Change

Scientists do not agree on what caused the little ice age, but the main reasons suggested are that the sun started giving off less heat and that there was an increase in volcanoes erupting. When volcanoes erupt, their ash blocks the sun's rays from reaching the ground and so the world isn't warmed as much.

What we do know is that the little ice age killed livestock and ruined crops, leading to famine (where there is no food over a large area of land) and disease. In the far north, the little ice age killed off the Viking population on Greenland.

WHERE IN THE WORLD
Across the whole Northern Hemisphere, particularly noticed where there were more people, such as in Europe.

ENGLAND
London •   GERMANY
FRANCE   EUROPE

Frozen Europe
Right: People on the frozen River Thames in London during the 17th century. Below: Traveling across frozen rivers and lakes became normal in winter in 19th-century Germany.

FACTS

• The European famine in 1315 killed 1.5 million people.

• This was a *mini* ice age. The last *major* ice age ended more than 10,000 years ago.

• During some winters, Londoners could cross the frozen River Thames and New Yorkers could walk across the ice in New York Harbor from Manhattan Island to Staten Island.

THE FORESTS OF EASTER ISLAND

From 1200 CE

Easter Island was once covered in 50 ft. (15 m)-high subtropical palm-tree forests where many seabirds nested. Both of these are now extinct.

Polynesian settlers cut the trees down for firewood and to clear land for farming, but scientists disagree on why the forests didn't grow back. Some believe that once the trees were cut down they couldn't grow again because of the weakened soil. Others believe that rats arrived on board ships and ate all the palm seeds, making it impossible for new trees to grow. Without the trees, there was nowhere for the birds to nest, and five species became extinct.

When European explorers arrived in the 18th century, more than 3,000 Polynesian people were living on the island but there weren't any trees.

Mystery Island

Early Polynesians built more than 800 giant stone statues. Neither the Easter Islanders nor scientists today know for sure how these statues were moved into place.

WHERE IN THE WORLD
Easter Island is in the Pacific Ocean, 2,180 mi. (3,510 km) west of Chile.

SOUTH AMERICA
PERU
PACIFIC OCEAN
Easter Island
CHILE

Isolated Island
Left: The stone statues on Easter Island were all carved at one quarry in an extinct volcano. Below: Ruins of the stone houses of Polynesian settlers on Easter Island.

FACTS

• It is one of the world's most isolated islands. The nearest neighbors are on Pitcairn Island, 1,289 mi. (2,075 km) away.

• The stone statues were carved from 1100 to 1680 CE. They represent dead family members worshipped as gods.

• In 1862, Peruvian slave raiders captured or killed 1,500 Easter Islanders—almost half the island's population.

• Due to diseases brought by the Europeans, by 1877 there were only 111 Easter Islanders left.

THE BLACK DEATH

WHEN: 1347–51

Caused by bacteria carried by fleas on rats (and then humans) from China, the Black Death was a plague that killed more than 75 million people.

The Black Death is thought to have started in the 1330s, carried along trade routes west. It was called the bubonic plague because of the swellings (known as "buboes") that appeared on people's bodies. Skin would turn black, the infected would develop a fever, and up to 75 percent of them would die within just a week.

Whole households and villages were wiped out. Half the people in the city of Paris died. When the healthy recognized that people were infected, they bricked up the infected in their homes so they could not spread the disease further.

Looking for Blame
The causes of the plague were unknown at the time. Blame was usually placed on non-Christians and foreigners.

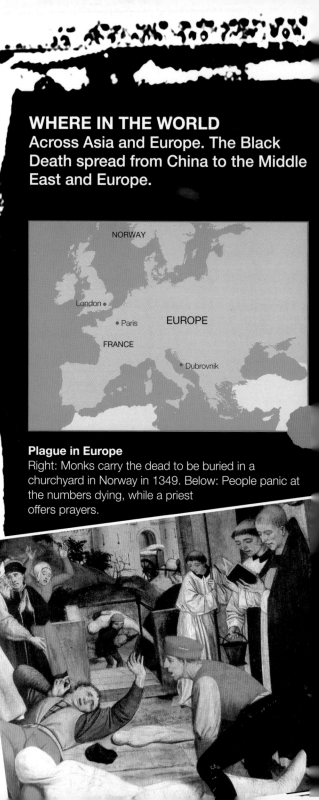

Plague in Europe
Right: Monks carry the dead to be buried in a churchyard in Norway in 1349. Below: People panic at the numbers dying, while a priest offers prayers.

FACTS

• The Black Death also killed about a third of the population in China.

• Earlier, the plague swept across Europe in the 6th and 7th centuries and appeared again in China and India in the 19th century.

• The people of Dubrovnik isolated ships that wanted to enter the port to see if they were carrying the Black Death. It is from this that we have the word quarantine, from the Italian words *quaranta giorni*, meaning "forty days"—the length of time the ships were isolated.

COLONIZATION OF THE AMERICAS

WHEN: 1493–1650

The Spanish conquests in the Caribbean and Central and South America led to the deaths of 45 million Native Americans.

The Spanish discovered the Americas by accident. They had been looking for a new sea route to India and China. But on finding the Americas, they began to build settlements and attacked the Native people.

In three years (1518–21), Hernán Cortés destroyed the Aztec empire, killing thousands of people. In the 1530s, the Incan civilization in Peru was crushed by Francisco Pizarro's armies.

The Bigger Killer

But even deadlier than the warriors were the diseases the Europeans brought with them. The common cold, influenza, measles, and cholera, among many others, were all diseases that hadn't existed in the Americas before. The Native Americans had no resistance to them. Smallpox killed three million Aztecs and more than 100,000 Incans in their capital, Cuzco. About 90 percent of the Native American people died.

WHERE IN THE WORLD
The Caribbean islands, Mexico, Central America, and northern South America.

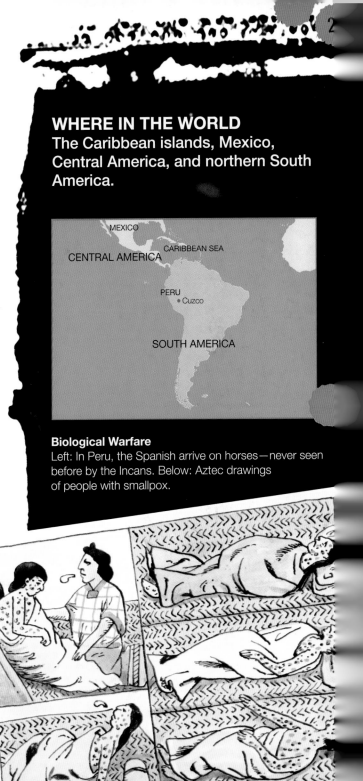

MEXICO

CENTRAL AMERICA

CARIBBEAN SEA

PERU
• Cuzco

SOUTH AMERICA

Biological Warfare
Left: In Peru, the Spanish arrive on horses—never seen before by the Incans. Below: Aztec drawings of people with smallpox.

FACTS

• Other diseases the Europeans took to America were leprosy, typhoid, and the bubonic plague.

• There were no cows, donkeys, horses, oranges, or coffee in the Americas before the Spanish introduced them.

• The Spanish brought back from America potatoes, tomatoes, turkeys, and chili peppers, among other plants and animals.

• The Spanish wanted to find a new sea route to the Indies because the Portuguese controlled the route around Africa.

SMALLPOX IN NORTH AMERICA

WHEN: 1617–1902

Although fighting and forcing them off their land killed many North American Indians, disease, in particular smallpox, was the biggest killer.

Around 1580, the British and French arrived in North America to set up their colonies. Along with their plans for the New World, they also brought their diseases, including smallpox. This caused flu-like symptoms before leading to vomiting and blisters appearing all over the body.

Many Europeans died from smallpox (about 400,000 a year in the 1700s), but they had built up some resistance over centuries of being exposed to the virus.

Deadly Virus

However, North American Indians had not been exposed to smallpox before, and in some places it killed 90 percent of the people. The population of the Massachusetts and Algonquin tribes was reduced from 30,000 to fewer than 500. Smallpox spread west and south across North America. By 1800, it had killed two-thirds of all Plains Indians, and by the early 20th century about one million Native Americans.

WHERE IN THE WORLD
Across North America, beginning in the northeast where the Europeans first settled.

GREAT PLAINS

NORTH AMERICA · Massachusetts

Continental Plague
Right: Wampanoags suffering from smallpox.
Below: Native American Chief Pontiac confronts British Colonel Henry Boquet, who had ordered his men to spread smallpox.

FACTS

• In 1796, an English doctor noticed that milkmaids who suffered from cowpox didn't suffer from smallpox. If people were injected with a small amount of the cowpox virus, their bodies developed a resistance against smallpox, which was more serious.

• The doctor called the material he injected a "vaccine," from the Latin *vacca* for cow, because it contained cowpox.

• In 1980, vaccinations for smallpox had wiped out the disease around the world.

GREAT FIRE OF LONDON

September 2–5, 1666

In London, a bakery fire caused the destruction of 13,000 homes, 87 parish churches, and the old St. Paul's Cathedral.

On the night of September 2, a fire broke out in a London bakery. The wind blew the fire westward, setting thatched roofs and wooden buildings ablaze across the city.

Making a Firestorm

The method of firefighting was to destroy houses in the path of the fire. That way the fire wouldn't be able to spread and would burn itself out. However, the Mayor of London, Sir Thomas Bloodworth, did not think the fire was serious enough and delayed pulling down housing. The wind built the fire into a raging inferno that burned for three days. Then, the winds died down and gunpowder was used to destroy houses and create a firebreak. Only four people are reported to have died, but it is probable that many more people died than was recorded.

WHERE IN THE WORLD
In London, England. The fire broke out in a road called Pudding Lane near London Bridge.

ENGLAND

London

Escaping the Fire
Left: London on fire. Flames surround the old St. Paul's Cathedral. Below: People climbed into boats on the River Thames to escape the fire.

FACTS

- The great fire destroyed 373 acres (150 hectares) of the city.

- It had been a dry summer, so rivers and ponds had less water in them for firefighting and the wooden houses burned more easily.

- In places, the fire leapt 100 ft. (32 m). Its smoke could be seen from Oxford, 54 mi. (87 km) away.

- One positive thing about the fire is that it killed many of London's rats, helping to fight the outbreak of bubonic plague.

LISBON EARTHQUAKE

November 1, 1755

Lisbon was shaken by a huge earthquake, followed by fires and three tsunamis. Portugal never completely recovered from the destruction.

By the middle of the 18th century, Portugal was a rich nation. Its capital, Lisbon, was a beautiful European port city of 275,000 people.

On the morning of November 1, 1755, an enormous earthquake shook the city. It was centered 120 mi. (193 km) southwest of Portugal in the Atlantic Ocean. About half an hour later, the first of three tsunamis slammed into Lisbon's harbor and central areas. Many people had taken to boats to escape the tremors on land, but they were lost at sea.

Burning Ruins

Where the city hadn't been affected by the tsunamis, fires broke out from overturned candles and cooking pots. The fire burned for five days, after which 85 percent of the city had been destroyed, and about 100,000 people were killed.

WHERE IN THE WORLD
Lisbon, the capital of Portugal in southwest Europe.

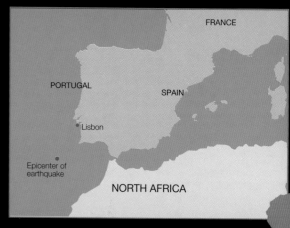

FRANCE

PORTUGAL   SPAIN

•Lisbon

Epicenter of
earthquake

NORTH AFRICA

Triple Disaster
Right: Lisbon on fire after the earthquake and tsunamis. Below: The people of Lisbon trying to help each other in the chaos.

FACTS

• Lisbon had been devastated by earlier earthquakes in 1344 and 1531 but had been rebuilt.

• The huge earthquake is thought to have measured well above 8.5 on the Richter scale.

• The Lisbon earthquake was caused by the underground movement of the African continental plate against the Eurasian continental plate. The plates move very slowly, pushing against each other, and this eventually causes earthquakes.

GREAT FIRE OF MOSCOW

September 14–18, 1812

The fire that destroyed three-quarters of Moscow was probably started deliberately by the Russians. But why would they set their own city ablaze?

In June 1812, Napoleon, the undefeated military leader of France, who had already conquered much of Europe invaded Russia. Instead of facing Napoleon's army in battle, the Russians retreated, drawing Napoleon's forces deeper into Russia and away from supply lines. As Napoleon reached Moscow, the Russians abandoned the city. Napoleon's exhausted army camped in the city, but on its first night fires broke out across Moscow.

A Terrible Trap

It seems that the Russians had set a trap: They had allowed Napoleon's forces to enter the city and then set fire to it. Too weak to escape the city, 20,000 of Napoleon's wounded soldiers died. The fire raged for five days, destroying the mainly wooden buildings. After that, Napoleon's soldiers began to starve in the empty city and he ordered a retreat to France. He had finally been defeated.

WHERE IN THE WORLD

Moscow, Russia. At the time, St. Petersburg, not Moscow, was the capital of Russia.

Firestorm City

Left: Napoleon's soldiers are caught in the center of the city with the fire burning all around them. Below: At the Kremlin in the heart of Moscow, Napoleon watches the fire rage.

FACTS

- The fire destroyed 122 of Moscow's 329 churches. The Russians defeated Napoleon but had sacrificed their city.

- Tchaikovsky's *1812 Overture* was composed to commemorate the defense of Russia.

- On Napoleon's retreat from Moscow, his soldiers suffered from frostbite, disease, starvation, and attacks from the Russians.

- By the time Napoleon's army reached safety in November, only 100,000 of the original 615,000 soldiers were alive.

MOUNT TAMBORA VOLCANO

WHERE IN THE WORLD
Mount Tambora is on Sumbawa Island, Indonesia, in southeast Asia, but people worldwide were affected by the eruption.

April 10, 1815

Lava and ash raining down might seem like the most destructive thing a volcano can do. But it can also change the climate, causing famine.

When the Tambora Volcano erupted, it blew 3,500 ft. (1,066 m) off the mountain, leaving a huge crater. A cloud of ash and rock was driven 28 mi. (44 km) into the air. Flows of superheated gas and fast-moving rock killed 11,000 people on Sumbawa and neighboring islands.

Ultimately, the ash thrown into the air reduced the amount of sunlight reaching the ground. Temperatures around the world dropped by up to 11.8°F (0.7°C). This created what was known as "the year without summer." Crops failed and there were famines throughout Southeast Asia.

Far-reaching Effect
It is calculated that 60,000 people died as a result of this eruption, most of whom were in the Indonesian islands. However, there were also famines as far away as North America and Europe.

CHINA
Hong Kong

Bangkok • SOUTHEAST ASIA

PHILIPPINES

Sumatra

INDONESIA
Mount Tambora

AUSTRALIA

Mountain That Blew Its Top Off
Right: Aerial view of Mount Tambora. The eruption blew off the top of the mountain, leaving a crater.
Below: A side view of the crater today.

FACTS

- The eruption of Mount Tambora was heard on Sumatra Island more than 1,200 mi. (1,930 km) away.

- As a consequence of the volcano, it snowed in New York State that summer.

- The ash particles in the air that summer turned the sunsets as far away as London brilliant pinks, oranges, and purples.

- The eruption was the largest and most destructive in recorded history.

IRISH POTATO FAMINE

WHEN: 1845–51

When a fungus ruined the potato crops in Ireland in the middle of the 1800s, about 1.5 million people died of starvation and disease.

In 1846, a fungus swept through all of Ireland's potato crop, resulting in famine. Irish farmers were only allowed to farm small plots of land, and often, potatoes were the only crop that could feed a whole family.

Although Britain was one of the richest countries in the world, its response to the famine was poor. One effort was to try to employ Irish people in workhouses, but the conditions were so bad that 200,000 workers died.

Relief Stopped

Relief was soon stopped because some in the British government felt that it was better for Irish farmers if the British didn't interfere. Others thought that the Irish were simply lazy and needed to be taught a lesson in looking after themselves.

WHERE IN THE WORLD
Ireland, western Europe. Ireland had been under British rule since 1807.

SCOTLAND

IRELAND • Dublin

GREAT BRITAIN

WALES

ENGLAND

London •

The Great Hunger
Left: Starving Irish people—some of them shoeless—on their way to England to find work. Below: A memorial to the victims of the famine in present-day Dublin.

FACTS

• The potato was the main food for half of the Irish population in the 1800s. Before the famine, two-thirds of Ireland's eight million people farmed land.

• The population in Ireland is still less than it was before the famine.

• Pushed by the effects of the famine, three million Irish people moved to the United States.

• The British Empire suffered a further major famine in India in 1876–79, when between six and ten million people died.

LIGHTNING STRIKE IN RHODES

April 3, 1856

A single bolt of lightning set a whole town on fire and killed almost 1,000 people.

Christian warriors who became known as the Knights of Rhodes settled on Rhodes in the 14th century. They built the Palace of the Grand Master and next to it the Church of St. John. In 1522, Rhodes was taken over by Ottoman Turks who were Muslims. They turned the church into a mosque and made the mistake of storing gunpowder in the bell tower. Tall buildings are much more likely to be hit by lightning, and in 1856 a bolt of lightning struck the bell tower. The gunpowder exploded and a fire started.

Town on Fire
To make matters worse, a storm blew in, whipped up the flames, and helped the fire jump from the church to the palace and then to the narrow streets and packed houses of the town below. That single lightning bolt caused a fire that killed more than 900 people.

WHERE IN THE WORLD
The city of Rhodes on Rhodes Island in the eastern Mediterranean Sea.

EUROPE

ITALY   GREECE

OTTOMAN EMPIRE

Athens

Rhodes

Crete

NORTH AFRICA

Lightning Strike
Right: The ruins of the Palace of the Grand Master and the Church of St. John after the lightning strike and fire. Below: The rebuilt Palace of the Grand Master today.

FACTS

• The odds of someone in the United States being struck by lightning in their life are 1 in 10,000.

• Although we think of lightning happening only with thunderstorms, lightning can strike 10 mi. (16 km) away in clear sky.

• It is estimated that 24,000 people around the world are killed by lightning strikes each year.

• In Australia in 2005, 68 cows ready for milking were killed by lightning when it struck the tree they were sheltering under.

GREAT CHICAGO FIRE

October 8–10, 1871

In 1871, a small fire whipped up by strong winds caused the deaths of an estimated 300 people and the loss of homes for 100,000 people.

The summer of 1871 had been very dry because there had been a quarter of the usual rainfall. On October 8, a small fire started in, or near, a barn on the west side of the Chicago River. Strong winds helped the fire jump from one wooden house to another and even across the Chicago River. In some places, the river was so polluted that the water caught fire.

Missing Bodies

The fire raged for two days before heavy rains helped it to burn itself out. The fire had destroyed an area 4 mi. (6 km) long and 1 mi. (1.6 km) wide. About 18,000 buildings were ruined. The official death toll was 125, but many bodies were never found. However, the fire had created a space in the center of the city to start again. In rebuilding, Chicago became a world leader in new steel architecture.

WHERE IN THE WORLD
Chicago, Illinois. Chicago is on the southwestern shores of Lake Michigan.

Lake Michigan • Chicago

USA

Windy City Fire
Left: Wind whipping the fire across the city.
Below: The ruins of the Field, Leiter & Co. store and the burned-out walls of the First National Bank building.

FACTS

• On the same day, there were three other major fires in towns along Lake Michigan.

• The Chicago riverside was badly hit because much of it was flammable: wooden warehouses, lumber yards, and fuel for ships.

• After the fire, the world's first skyscraper was built in Chicago in 1885.

• The word Chicago originally comes from the Native American Miami-Illinois word *shikaakwa*, which means "wild onion."

KRAKATOA VOLCANO

August 27, 1883

One of the most violent volcanoes in history, the 1883 eruption on the island of Krakatoa was heard 2,891 mi. (4,653 km) away.

Krakatoa had once been 6,000 ft. (1,828 m) high, but previous eruptions had already blasted away more than half of the mountain. On August 27, a massive eruption almost completely destroyed the island.

Flying Ash and Rock

A huge pillar of ash reached 50 mi. (80 km) into the sky. The explosion threw out 5 cubic mi. (21 cubic km) of rock. The pumice floating on the water was so thick that patches were large enough to carry people and stop ships.

The eruption also caused an enormous tsunami 120 ft. (36 m) high. The coastlines of Java and Sumatra were hit by huge waves that killed more than 36,000 people and carried massive blocks of coral weighing as much as 600 tons (544 metric tons). Today the area is still volcanic, but it is very unlikely to have such a big eruption again.

WHERE IN THE WORLD
The island of Krakatoa, between the islands of Sumatra and Java, in Southeast Asia.

CHINA
Hong Kong
Bangkok
PHILIPPINES
Sumatra
INDONESIA
Krakatoa
Java
AUSTRALIA

Wave of Destruction
Right: Tidal increases were reported as far away as South America. Below: The steamer ship *Beroux* was deposited in the middle of the Indonesian jungle by the tsunami.

FACTS

• An area of more than 300,000 sq. mi. (800,000 sq. km) was affected by the ash.

• The Krakatoa volcano was so powerful that pressure waves were picked up on every barometer around the world.

• After the eruption of the volcano, spectacular sunsets were seen all around the world.

• As a result of ash in the atmosphere blocking out the sun, global temperatures went down by 2.6°F (1.2°C).

SAN FRANCISCO EARTHQUAKE

April 18, 1906

On April 18, the San Andreas Fault shifted along 267 mi. (430 km) of its length, with the earthquake's epicenter beneath San Francisco.

The 45-second earthquake struck at 5:12 AM. The quake registered 7.7 on the Richter scale, and in places the ground moved 20 ft. (6 m). In those few seconds, the city was ruined: buildings collapsed, water mains split and people were killed in their homes and on the streets.

City on Fire

However, worse was to come. The quake broke the gas lines, which caught fire. For three days, the fire destroyed 4.7 square mi. (12.1 sq. km) of the city before it was eventually brought under control.

The earthquake and the fire caused massive devastation. It destroyed 28,188 buildings, killed about 3,000 people, and a further 225,000 people were left homeless. The cost of the damage at the time was $400 million. It was the largest geological disaster in America's history.

WHERE IN THE WORLD

San Francisco, California. San Francisco stands on the San Andreas Fault line that runs down through California.

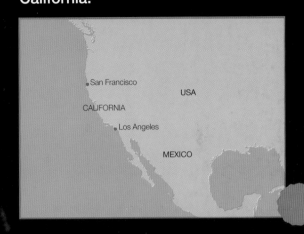

Earthquake Aftermath
Left: The Palace Hotel was designed to survive earthquakes; it survived the earthquake but was burned to a shell by the fire. Below: Buildings leaning after the quake.

FACTS

- The majority of the houses that collapsed were made of wood. Brick buildings were more stable in the quake.

- In Monterey County, the earthquake permanently shifted the course of the Salinas River.

- After the earthquake, Los Angeles overtook San Francisco as the main city on the west coast of the United States.

- Scientists believe that the San Andreas Fault has a major quake every 200 years. The next one is due around 2106.

THE SINKING OF THE *TITANIC*

April 14–15, 1912

The largest ship afloat at the time, the *Titanic* sank after hitting an iceberg on her first voyage. Many people lost their lives.

On April 10, 1912, the *Titanic* set sail from Southampton, England bound for New York City with 2,224 passengers and crew on board.

On April 14, other ships radioed the *Titanic* to warn them of icebergs. Only the first of three messages reached the *Titanic*'s captain, who changed course to head further south and avoid icebergs.

That night, a lookout spotted an iceberg. The *Titanic* tried to change course, but it was too late to turn such a big ship. The iceberg tore into the ship's hull and water began flooding in.

"Iceberg right ahead!"

The ship was soon sinking but there were only enough lifeboats for just over half of the people on board. Within two hours and 40 minutes, the *Titanic* had sunk. Many drowned when it sank or died of hypothermia in the freezing water.

WHERE IN THE WORLD

Titanic sank 375 mi. (600 km) south of Newfoundland in the Atlantic Ocean.

GREENLAND

ICELAND

CANADA

Newfoundland

Great Britain

Southampton

USA

New York

Site of sinking of the *Titanic*

Rusting Wreck

Right: The *Titanic* hits an iceberg and sinks. Below: The wreck lies 12,000 ft. (3,700 m) deep. Bacteria will eventually reduce the ship to just a patch of rust on the seabed.

FACTS

- The order on the *Titanic* was to save "women and children first"; 90 percent of the people who died were men.

- As many as 500 lives could have been saved if the lifeboats had been launched when they were full.

- The *Titanic* was not breaking the law by not having enough lifeboats for everyone. The law was changed after the disaster.

- Two hours after the *Titanic* sank, the SS *Carpathia* arrived and rescued the 700 survivors waiting in lifeboats.

THE GROUNDING OF THE SS *MAKAMBO*

June 15, 1918

We might think that there are rats everywhere, but there were once no black rats on Lord Howe Island, and their arrival caused an environmental disaster.

In June 1918, the passenger and cargo ship SS *Makambo* ran aground on Lord Howe Island. Black rats from the ship managed to reach land, where they ate crops as well as lizards, snails, and beetles.

Dying Species

The rats ate both the birds and the birds' eggs, and they eventually killed five species of birds found only on the island, including the Lord Howe thrush and the Lord Howe starling, which became extinct.

To deal with the rats, masked owls were brought to the island to eat them. However, this just made the problem worse: the Lord Howe boobook bird (another kind of owl) then became extinct, too. There are still black rats on the island today.

WHERE IN THE WORLD
Lord Howe Island, in the Pacific Ocean between Australia and New Zealand.

AUSTRALIA

• Lord Howe Island

• Sydney

Tasmania

NEW ZEALAND

Rat Attack
Left: Lord Howe Island today. The island was once volcanic. Below: Black rats hiding in a ship's hull.

FACTS

• Despite five bird species becoming extinct, Lord Howe Island is still an excellent place for spotting rare birds.

• The Lord Howe flax snail is also now rare because of the introduction of black rats.

• The Lord Howe Island stick insect was also thought to be extinct by 1940, but in 2001 some were found on a neighboring island.

• Lord Howe Island was not discovered by humans until 1788.

INFLUENZA PANDEMIC

WHEN: 1918–19

We might expect the biggest killer of 1918 to have been World War I (1914–18), but flu swept around the world, killing around 70 million people.

A pandemic is a disease that affects many people around the world. However, what became the influenza pandemic was first noticed in American and British soldiers fighting in France in the final year of World War I. The soldiers were weakened by war, and within months the flu virus was causing more serious illnesses. Around 30 percent of those affected died.

Global Killer

The disease soon spread beyond soldiers. More than 400,000 German townspeople died, but in poorer countries the effects were worse. In India, 16 million people died. Surprisingly, it was not the elderly who were most likely to die but adults aged between 20 and 40. Many people went from being perfectly healthy to dead within 24 hours. Then, toward the end of 1919, the pandemic faded away.

WHERE IN THE WORLD
Worldwide. The disease probably originated in China but was first noticed among soldiers fighting in World War I in France.

• FRANCE
• USA
CHINA

Fighting the Flu
Right: A military hospital in Kansas during the influenza pandemic. Below: People wore masks to help protect them from the flu virus. It was not always effective.

FACTS

• This influenza was often called Spanish Flu because it was most intense in Spain, and Spain was the first country to report it.

• The most common cause of death was suffocation from pneumonia.

• 43,000 American servicemen in Europe died of flu in 1918–19.

• To try to stop the spread of the disease in the United States, people were not allowed to travel. Gatherings, such as funerals, could last for only 15 minutes.

THE CLARENDON
SOFT DRINKS
GARS ACCO
INFLUENZA

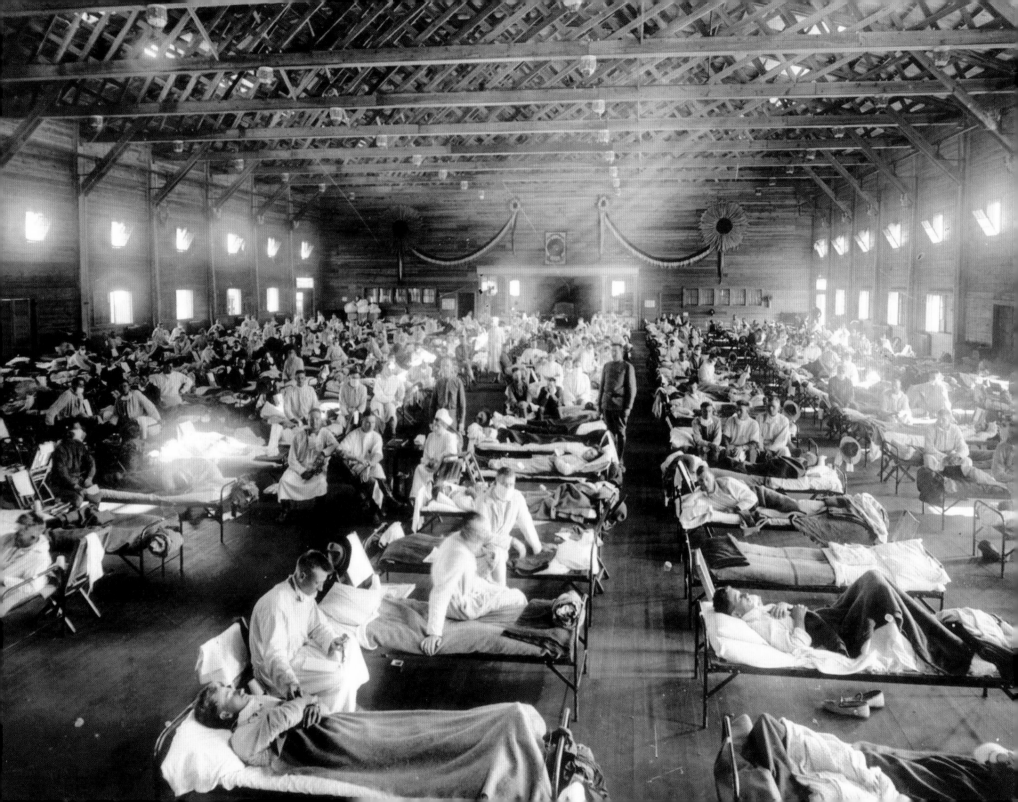

U.S. SUPER TORNADO OUTBREAK

March 18, 1925

The people of the American Midwest deal with tornadoes every spring, but the one in 1925 remains the nation's worst tornado disaster.

At around 1 PM on March 18, the skies northwest of Ellington, Missouri, darkened into a storm system. A cold front from the southwest was mixing with moist air from the Gulf of Mexico—perfect weather for creating a tornado.

Turned Upside Down

For three and a half hours, the tornado carved its way across Missouri, Illinois, and Indiana. At its height, it was about 1 mi. (1.6 km) wide and moved at an average speed of 63 mph (100 km/h). But inside, it was twisting at 300 mph (482 km/h). Houses were turned on their sides and people were hit by lethal debris. Entire towns were wiped out.

After 219 mi. (352 km), the tornadoes fizzled out, leaving a path of terrible destruction. The outbreak killed 695 people, injured more than 2,000, and destroyed more than 15,000 homes.

WHERE IN THE WORLD
From Ellington, Missouri, across Illinois to Petersburg, Indiana, USA.

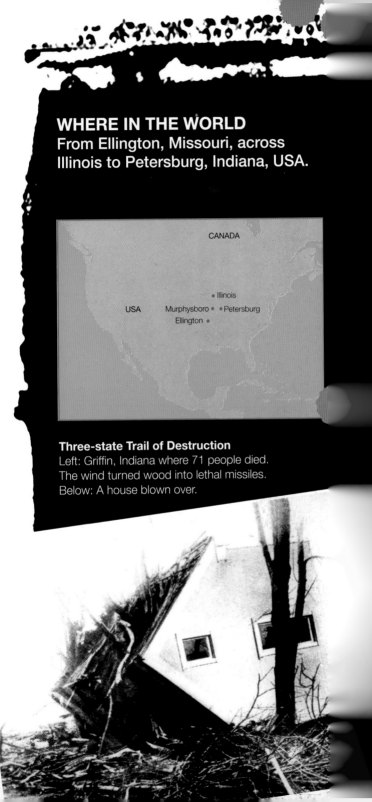

CANADA

USA   Illinois   Murphysboro • • Petersburg   Ellington •

Three-state Trail of Destruction
Left: Griffin, Indiana where 71 people died. The wind turned wood into lethal missiles. Below: A house blown over.

FACTS

• It was recorded as an F5 tornado—the most powerful classification of tornado.

• The tornado took only 40 minutes to cross Illinois, but it killed 600 people and injured nearly 1,500.

• There were other tornados that day in Tennessee, Kentucky, Alabama, and Kansas.

• Eyewitnesses described it as: "rolling fog or boiling clouds on the ground."

YELLOW RIVER FLOOD

WHEN: 1931

When the Yellow River burst its banks in 1931, the floods, loss of crops, famine, and disease killed 3.7 million people.

The Yellow River in China is 3,000 mi. (4,800 km) long. It carries a high volume of silt (particles of minerals, sand, and clay), turning the water a muddy yellow, which is how the river gets its name. If the silt builds up on the riverbed, it causes the river to overflow its banks. This is what happened in 1931 after a long period of drought was followed by heavy rainstorms. Crops were washed away and cities were flooded.

Breaking Dams

The Huai River and the Yangtze River also overflowed their banks. Up to 140,000 people were killed by the actual floodwaters. However, the flood destroyed crops and eventually caused famine. With the bodies of dead people and animals floating in the waters, diseases spread quickly, too. The more people who died, the more corpses there were to spread diseases.

Cities Submerged
Right: Shopping at markets was often done in waist-deep water. Below: Streets in the city of Hankow under water. Hankow stands where the Han and Yangtze rivers meet.

FACTS

• The Yellow River flooded 42,000 sq. mi. (108,000 square km) of land.

• In August, in the city of Hankow, water levels were 53 ft. (16 m) higher than normal.

• An earlier Yellow River flood that began in September, 1887 killed 900,000 people.

• In 1938, the Chinese decided to deliberately make the Yellow River flood to try to delay the advance of invading Japanese soldiers.

SOVIET UNION FAMINE

WHEN: 1932–33

More than six million people died in a famine caused by the Soviet government changing the way farming was organized.

To become a modern country like Germany, the United States, and Great Britain, the Soviet Union realized that it needed to become industrialized—that meant having factories, not just farms. The land was no longer owned by the farmers. It was owned by huge corporations and the government owned the crops.

The change was badly organized and the new farms produced just over half as much as they used to.

Flight to the Cities

Grain that was needed to feed the people was being sold abroad to buy machinery for the new factories. The result was famine. Millions of starving peasants headed to the cities to look for food, but died on the streets. If anyone stole from the farms, they were executed or sent to labor camps. Historians believe that the famine was used by Stalin to crush the Ukrainian people.

WHERE IN THE WORLD
Ukraine, southern Russia, and Kazakhstan in the former Soviet Union

USSR
Ukraine
• Kiev
Kazakhstan
Black Sea
Caspian Sea
• Istanbul
TURKEY

Starving Farmers
Left: Starving peasants camp out on city streets. Below: A child suffering from malnourishment.

FACTS

• Passports were introduced to stop starving peasants moving from the countryside to the city in search of food.

• Until 1991, the Soviet Union didn't admit that the famine of 1932–33 had happened.

• It is estimated that five million people died in an earlier Russian famine in 1921.

• In 1946–47, the Soviet Union suffered another famine. It was caused by drought, but the loss of men and farm horses in World War II (1939–45) made it worse.

THE DUST BOWL

The Dust Bowl damaged millions of acres of farmland and caused hundreds of thousands of people to abandon their homes.

The dust storms of the 1930's were an agricultural disaster. A severe drought that began in 1930 dried out the top soil. The deep-rooted grasses that held the prairie soil together and kept moisture in were damaged by combine harvesters. Without these grasses to anchor the soil, it dried up. Once strong winds started, there was nothing to keep the soil in place and it blew away, destroying any chance of farming.

Great Depression

With their farms ruined, people abandoned their homes. By 1940, 2.5 million people had moved out of the Plains states. Around 200,000 people moved to California, but as the country was already suffering an economic depression, there were few opportunities for work.

WHERE IN THE WORLD
The prairies of the U.S., especially the states of Oklahoma, Texas, Kansas, Colorado, and New Mexico.

CANADA

USA   Great Plains
Colorado
          Kansas
             • Oklahoma City
Los Angeles   Oklahoma
      New Mexico
                Texas

The Dirty Thirties
Right: People in the town of Elkhart, Kansas watch as a dust storm approaches in 1937. Below: A car and carriages buried by the storms.

FACTS

• Some people died when the dust poisoned their lungs. Others starved.

• The farmers had not practiced crop rotation, where each year a different crop is farmed in a field. This stops the soil from becoming exhausted.

• Some of the land never fully recovered from this disaster.

• More than 220 million trees were planted across 18,600 mi. (29,900 km) of the Great Plains to help bind the soil again.

HINDENBURG DISASTER

May 6, 1937

The *Hindenburg* made several successful trips across the Atlantic Ocean before disaster brought the age of the airship to an end.

Unlike American airships, the German *Hindenburg* gained its lift from hydrogen gas rather than helium gas. Helium at the time could only be produced in the United States, and America had banned its export. Hydrogen, unlike helium, is highly flammable (will easily burn or catch fire).

On May 3, the *Hindenburg* took off from Frankfurt, Germany. On approaching its destination in New Jersey three days later, flames were spotted at the rear of the airship.

Then, the whole craft burst into a fireball. Within 37 seconds the entire ship was reduced to a burned-out skeleton.

Static Electricity

Incredibly, 62 people managed to escape by jumping to safety; another 35 died in the fire. The actual cause of the fire is unknown, but it is possible the airship's wet mooring lines created static sparks when they touched the station.

WHERE IN THE WORLD

Having crossed the Atlantic Ocean from Germany, the airship tried to dock at Lakehurst Naval Air Station, New Jersey.

New Jersey

USA

ATLANTIC OCEAN

Nightmare in the Sky
Left: The burnt-out remains of the *Hindenburg* minutes after it docked. Below: Before the disaster, the captain had taken a small detour to fly his passengers over Manhattan.

FACTS

- After the *Hindenburg* disaster, airplanes became the main form of air travel.

- The *Hindenburg* became lighter as it burned fuel. To keep its weight even, gutters were added to collect rainwater.

- In 1935, the *Hindenburg* had transported 2,600 people between Frankfurt, New York, and Rio de Janeiro, Brazil.

- The *Hindenburg* could carry 50 passengers and 61 crew members.

THE GREAT LONDON SMOG

December 5–9, 1952

The mixture of London winter weather and air pollution led to the deaths of thousands of people in one week.

In the early 1950s in London, England, people burned coal to warm their homes; there were also three coal-fired power stations in the city, and cars and buses added to the air pollution. On December 5, the wind was calm, the weather was cold, and a layer of polluted clouds (smog) sat over the city. This cloud stopped any fresh air getting in or any polluted air from escaping. Visibility was so bad that buses stopped running, and in some places people could not see 3 ft. (1 m) in front of them. The smog even crept into movie theaters, making the screens invisible.

Lung Infections

The smog lifted after four days, but many died from lung infections. It is now thought that as many as 12,000 people may have died from the smog.

WHERE IN THE WORLD
London, England. The smog dispersed when winds picked up and blew it out into the North Sea.

ENGLAND

NORTH SEA

London

FRANCE

Toxic Darkness
Right: Piccadilly Circus in the center of London during the Great London Smog. Below: People wear face masks to try to protect them against breathing in the poisonous air.

FACTS

• Many people used a cheaper type of coal that produced toxic sulfur dioxide in the smoke.

• The fogs were called "pea soupers" because of the thick, yellowy color produced by the sulfur dioxide.

• As a result of the Great Smog of 1952, the British government decided to introduce new laws to try to clean up the air.

• This was the worst air pollution event that had occurred in the history of the United Kingdom.

GREAT CHINESE FAMINE

WHEN: 1958–61

The greatest manmade disaster in history, the Chinese famine of 1958–61 left people so hungry they resorted to eating grass and tree bark.

In the 1950s, China was still a country of farmers. To compete, Chinese leader Mao Tse Tung wanted to make farms produce more food and allow farm workers to move to factory work.

Manmade Catastrophe

The farmers planted a lot of seeds per field so that more crops would grow. However, the seeds were tightly packed and the crops didn't grow properly. Another plan was to kill off birds that ate the crops. But the birds also ate the insects that spoil crops. In addition, there were other problems, including floods in one area and a lack of rain in another. The result was a crop failure and a famine. It is estimated that 45 million people died during the famine.

WHERE IN THE WORLD
Throughout China.

SOVIET UNION

Beijing

Yellow River

NORTH KOREA

SOUTH KOREA

JAPAN

CHINA

Hong Kong

Rice Rescue
Left: People collect sacks of emergency rice.
Below: Flour to be distributed to the starving is unloaded from a ship in Kowloon Harbor, Hong Kong.

FACTS

• The Chinese had been influenced by Soviet scientist Trofim Lysenko. Later, it was realized that he'd faked his results.

• Mao Tse Tung had thousands of starving people executed because he claimed they had been hiding rice.

• As part of Communist rule, farms were no longer owned by individual farmers but joined together in big collectives.

• Despite this famine, Cambodia, Ethiopia, and North Korea tried similar farming methods and created their own famines.

THE DRYING UP OF THE ARAL SEA

1960s – present

Once the fourth-largest lake in the world, the Aral Sea is now only one-tenth its size after its water was diverted for farming.

In the 1960s, Soviet scientists decided to take water from rivers flowing into the Aral Sea and use it to water cotton fields in the desert in Uzbekistan. The scientists did this knowing that it would ruin the Aral Sea. Uzbekistan's cotton industry succeeded, but as the Aral Sea shrank, the water became too salty for animals and plant life to survive.

Today, the Aral Sea is divided into three lakes. The dried-up seabed released salt and toxic chemicals that blow across the surrounding land, causing cancers and lung diseases in people.

Climate Change

The climate has changed: summers are hotter and drier, winters are colder and longer. There is unemployment because there is no longer a fishing industry. However, attempts are now being made to bring water back to the Aral Sea.

WHERE IN THE WORLD
Between Kazakhstan and Uzbekistan in the former Soviet Union.

Kazakhstan
Aral Sea
Uzbekistan

Dry Seabed
Right: Boats left high and dry when the Aral Sea dried up. Below: The separate lakes in this satellite image of the Aral Sea were all once part of the same body of water.

FACTS

• The huge amount of water that has been lost from the Aral Sea was the equivalent of draining both Lake Ontario and Lake Erie.

• The Aral Sea is now saltier than the Dead Sea in the Middle East.

• There are graveyards of rusting ships left on the Aral Sea's dried-up seabed.

• The Owens Valley in California dried up after water was channeled to supply the city of Los Angeles in 1913.

BANGLADESH CYCLONE

November 12, 1970

Every year tropical cyclones hit Bangladesh, but the deadliest on record came in 1970, when winds of 124 mph (200 km/h) tore into the country.

Flooding is common in Bangladesh. It is a low-lying country where huge rivers such as the Ganges spread out like fans into deltas before they reach the Indian Ocean. Many people live in wooden houses raised on stilts and embankments to keep them off the ground if there is a flood. But on November 12, a cyclone knocked down thousands of these houses.

However, the winds also caused a rise in the sea level that drove a 23 ft. (7 m) wall of water inland. This ruined crops, wrecked houses, and drowned people and livestock.

Dirty Water

That night 500,000 people were killed. Hundreds of thousands more were left homeless. And the storm had also spread sewage water into the clean water supplies. Many people died from dirty-water diseases, such as cholera and typhus.

WHERE IN THE WORLD
The low-lying flatlands and river deltas of Bangladesh, south Asia.

PAKISTAN

BANGLADESH

INDIA

Storm Damage
Left: A family looks at the wreckage of their wood-frame house. Below: With smaller bodies, children suffer more severely from malnourishment and diseases.

FACTS

• In 1991, another tropical cyclone killed 138,000 people in Bangladesh and left 10 million homeless.

• A tropical cyclone is a storm system with a spiral of thunderstorms that produce strong winds and heavy rain.

• At the time, Bangladesh was called East Pakistan and was part of Pakistan. Many people felt that the Pakistani government didn't do enough to help after the disaster. The following year Bangladesh went to war against Pakistan and won independence.

MOUNT ST. HELENS VOLCANO

May 18, 1980

There have been volcanoes that killed many more people than Mount St. Helens, but this is the deadliest in the U.S. and caused mass destruction.

An earthquake measuring 5.1 on the Richter scale set off a debris avalanche of rocks, soil, and timber on the mountain. As the face of the mountain slid away, the molten rock in the volcano was exposed. The volcanic rock burst out, even overtaking the avalanche on the surface. The blast and the avalanche melted glaciers and caused floods. Mudflows spread up to 50 mi. (80 km) away.

Destructive Ash

There were 57 people killed; most suffocated by breathing in hot volcanic ash. The destruction was not only to lives but included 250 homes, 47 bridges, 15 mi. (24 km) of railways, and 185 mi. (298 km) of highway. About 7,000 big game animals (deer, elk, and bear) were killed. Wheat, apples, and potato crops were all destroyed by the heavy ash fall.

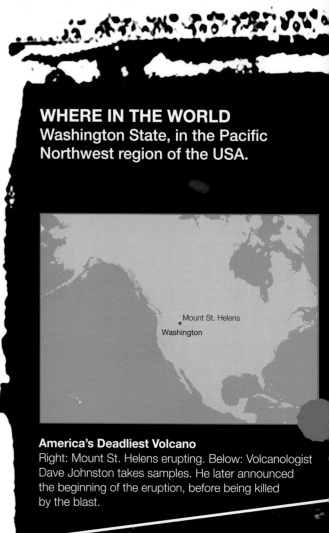

WHERE IN THE WORLD
Washington State, in the Pacific Northwest region of the USA.

Mount St. Helens

Washington

America's Deadliest Volcano
Right: Mount St. Helens erupting. Below: Volcanologist Dave Johnston takes samples. He later announced the beginning of the eruption, before being killed by the blast.

FACTS

• Mount St. Helens was closed to climbers between 2004 and 2006 because the volcano showed signs of new activity.

• There are 169 volcanoes in the United States; 18 of them are active. The rest are extinct or dormant (inactive).

• Active volcanoes in the U.S. are found on the west coast from California to Alaska and in Hawaii.

• Although destructive at first, the ash from the volcano is in the long run a good nutrient for the soil.

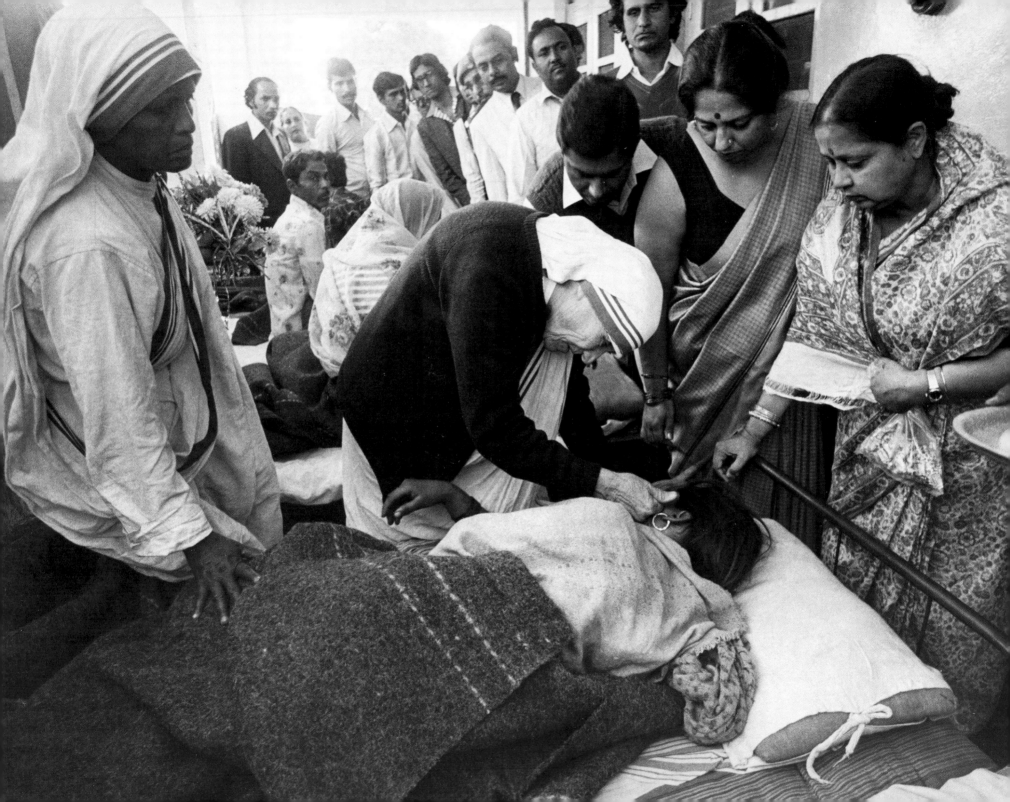

BHOPAL CHEMICAL BLAST

December 2–4, 1984

When an accident at a pesticide factory caused an explosion, many people were killed or blinded, and many years later others still suffer.

Union Carbide India Limited (UCIL) built a factory for making pesticides in the city of Bhopal, India. By the 1980s, the factory was no longer running, but it still contained many chemicals. One night, water was allowed to flow into a chemical tank, causing a massive explosion. The toxic gas spread across the city. People woke up choking and their eyes burning. Some people suffocated and others died when the gas attacked their nervous systems. Many were blinded. Within seven days up to 15,000 people had died.

Choking Gas

However, the disaster was not over. Although the gas blew away after a week, people continue to suffer in Bhopal from breathing problems, brain illnesses, and cancers caused by the blast.

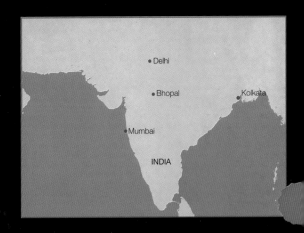

Toxic Spill
Left: Mother Teresa of Calcutta visits the injured in Bhopal. Below: Two people help a victim leave the factory site where the leak happened.

FACTS

• After the explosion, mercury levels in the water supply were six million times normal levels.

• Apart from the 15,000 people killed, another 120,000 developed serious health problems.

• What caused the water to enter the chemical tank isn't known. Most people think it was a mistake by a worker.

• Seven people were convicted for causing the deaths of so many.

CHERNOBYL EXPLOSION

April 26, 1986

It is calculated that the effects of the 1986 Chernobyl nuclear power plant explosion will last for 100 years.

In April 1986, a worker at the Chernobyl nuclear plant made a mistake, causing the reactor to overheat. An explosion blasted the concrete lid off the reactor and started a fire. More than 30 times the amount of radiation in the atomic bombs at Hiroshima and Nagasaki was released into the atmosphere. Higher levels of radiation were recorded across most of Europe. The people in the nearby town of Pripyat weren't warned of any danger, but after a few hours they began to feel ill.

Radiation Effects

Radiation poisoning killed 31 people over the next three weeks, but 2,500 may have died from the effects and many more developed cancers. In 2010 in Norway 950 mi. (1,528 km) away, livestock were being fed purified food because the grass was contaminated with radiation.

WHERE IN THE WORLD

In Ukraine, at that time in the Soviet Union. The radiation cloud spread over Ukraine, Belarus, and southern Russia.

NORWAY

GERMANY

Belarus

EUROPE

• Moscow

SOVIET UNION

• Chernobyl

Ukraine

Checking for Radiation
Left: Shortly after the explosion, smoke can still be seen coming from the reactor, but radiation itself is invisible. Below: Cars are checked with Geiger counters for radiation levels.

FACTS

• Victims said the radiation tasted like metal and they felt a tingling sensation on their faces.

• Abandoned by people, the forests around Chernobyl have spread and the numbers of wild animals have increased.

• In the Ukraine after the disaster, there was a big increase in the number of farm animals born with deformities.

• It is still forbidden to live within 19 mi. (30 km) of Chernobyl.

LIMNIC ERUPTION AT LAKE NYOS

August 21, 1986

Beneath Lake Nyos in Cameroon, Africa, lies an inactive volcano that still releases carbon dioxide gas into the lake.

Carbon dioxide dissolves into water, but an earthquake or landslide can unsettle the water, causing what is known as a limnic eruption, where the carbon dioxide suddenly comes out of the water solution. On August 21, 1986, 1.57 million tons of carbon dioxide burst out of Lake Nyos. Carbon dioxide is heavier than air and so the gas hugged the landscape, sweeping over many villages.

Gas Attack

The gas moved at up to 31 mph (50 km/h) over 16 mi. (25 km), suffocating villagers and 3,500 animals in its path. Survivors remembered choking and falling unconscious. About 4,000 villagers managed to escape the area, but they suffered breathing problems because of the gas. Since the disaster, a pipe has been installed to control the release of carbon dioxide from the lake.

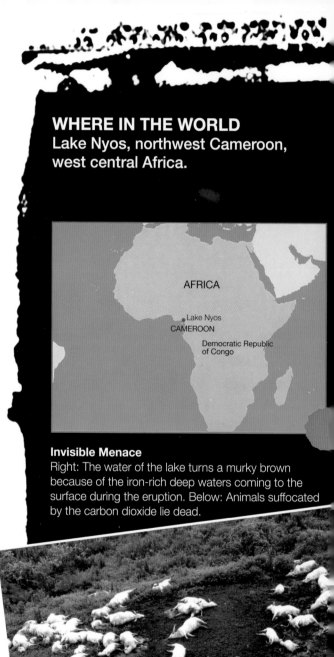

WHERE IN THE WORLD
Lake Nyos, northwest Cameroon, west central Africa.

AFRICA

Lake Nyos
CAMEROON
Democratic Republic of Congo

Invisible Menace
Right: The water of the lake turns a murky brown because of the iron-rich deep waters coming to the surface during the eruption. Below: Animals suffocated by the carbon dioxide lie dead.

FACTS

• The only other two known exploding lakes are both in Africa: Lake Monoun, also in Cameroon, and Lake Kivu in the Democratic Republic of Congo.

• Carbon dioxide is injected into soft drinks to give them their fizz.

• The eruption caused a 16 ft. (5 m) tsunami on the lake that damaged or destroyed vegetation on the banks.

• The eruption at Lake Nyos was the first known large-scale suffocation caused by a natural event.

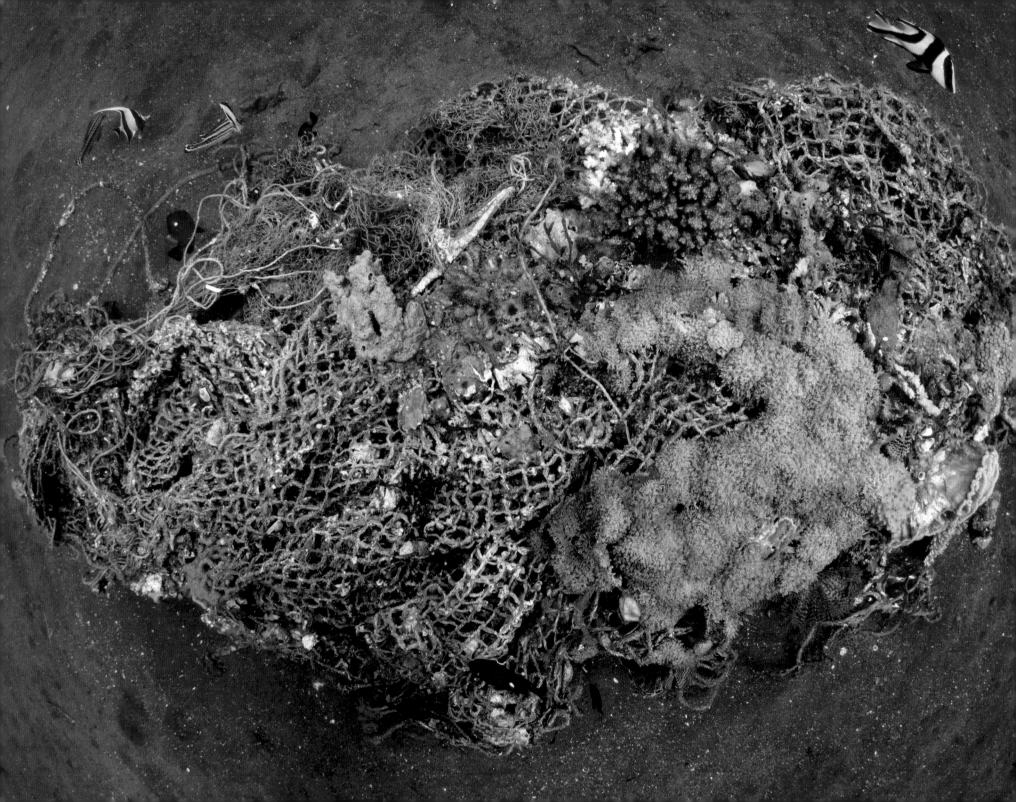

PACIFIC GARBAGE PATCH

Since 1988

Sea currents have gathered a mass of garbage from North America and Japan that now floats in the middle of the Pacific Ocean.

Although there are some larger pieces, most of the garbage cannot be seen by aircraft because it is made of smaller particles of plastic that are often underwater. The plastics slowly break down to smaller sizes. The patch does not move around much because it is in still water. The exact size of the patch is unknown, and estimates vary between 270,000 sq. mi. (700,000 sq. km) and 5,800,000 sq. mi. (15,000,000 sq. km).

Deadly Plastic

The plastics cannot be digested by birds and turtles, so many are killed each year. The plastics also absorb toxins. If the plastic is eaten by a fish, it is not only harmful to the fish, but the toxins can harm any animal that eats the fish, including humans.

WHERE IN THE WORLD
In the Pacific Ocean, north of Hawaii. The garbage gathers because the currents are weak.

USA

• Hawaii

PACIFIC OCEAN

SOUTH AMERICA

Floating Trash
Left: A mass of netting and other garbage that has joined together in the Pacific Ocean. Below: A water sample showing the generally small pieces of plastic that a fish can eat.

FACTS

• Similar patches of floating garbage are found in the Atlantic Ocean and in the Indian Ocean.

• It is not known how long it takes for a plastic bag to decay, but it could be more than 500 years.

• Since 1992, more than 28,000 bath toys have been floating around the world's oceans after falling off cargo ships.

• Garbage takes about one year to reach the Pacific patch from Asia and six years from North America.

EXXON VALDEZ OIL SPILL

March 24, 1989

Some disasters affect animals more than they do people. Seabird, fish, otter, and seal populations were devastated by the *Exxon Valdez* oil spill.

Taking oil from Alaska to California, the captain of the *Exxon Valdez* tanker steered the ship out of the port of Valdez, then left the third mate in charge. However, the radar wasn't working and the third mate didn't spot a rocky reef ahead. Also, the crew was overworked and tired. The tanker crashed into the reef, spilling more than 260,000 barrels of crude oil. The spill covered 1,300 mi. (2,100 km) of coastline and 11,000 square mi. (28,000 square km) of ocean.

Poison Sea

More than 100,000 seabirds, 2,800 sea otters, 300 harbor seals, 240 bald eagles, 22 orcas, and billions of salmon and herring eggs were killed. Sea birds died because the oil on their feathers didn't keep them warm and so they froze to death.

In the longer term, salmon didn't grow to be as large, whale populations moved away, and sea otters and ducks lived shorter lives.

WHERE IN THE WORLD
Off Prince William Sound in the Pacific Ocean off Alaska.

RUSSIA

Alaska

Prince William Sound

CANADA

Environmental Damage
Right: The *Exxon Valdez*. After the accident, the ship was repaired, renamed, and put back into service.
Below: Crude oil pollution at Rocky Point, Prince William Sound.

FACTS

- In 2007, it was calculated that 26,000 gallons of oil remained in the sandy soil on the Alaskan shoreline.

- Some fishing businesses on the Alaskan coast were ruined and fewer tourists wanted to visit that part of Alaska.

- It was the largest oil spill in U.S. waters until 2010's Deepwater Horizon disaster in the Gulf of Mexico, which spilled more than 4.5 million barrels of oil until it was capped in September 2010.

INDIAN OCEAN TSUNAMI

December 26, 2004

In December 2004, an underwater earthquake in the Indian Ocean was so big that it caused the Earth to wobble on its axis.

Measuring 9.0 on the Richter scale, the earthquake made the sea floor shift upward by several feet. This pushed water up creating a tsunami, which spread out across the Indian Ocean. As it neared land, the waves reached heights of 32–50 ft. (10–15 m). Within 15 minutes, the first wave hit the island of Sumatra. It swept away thousands of people and wiped entire coastal regions off the map. Over the next seven hours, tsunami waves hit coastlines in Somalia, 4,500 mi. (7,241 km) away.

Death Toll

The death toll was more than 250,000, but it also destroyed farms, coastlines, and communities. In Sri Lanka, thousands of rice, mango, and banana plantations were destroyed by the waves, which deposited salt water.

WHERE IN THE WORLD

The island of Sumatra in Indonesia, Thailand, Sri Lanka, southeast India, Bangladesh, Myanmar, Maldives, Malaysia, and Somalia.

INDIA
THAILAND
SOMALIA
SRI LANKA
Sumatra
MALDIVES
INDONESIA
INDIAN OCEAN

Megathrust Earthquake
Left: Ruined buildings on Phi Phi Island, Thailand, four days after the tsunami. Below: Damage at Velankanni Tamil Nadu, southeastern India.

FACTS

- This was one of the longest earthquakes, lasting between 8 to 10 minutes.

- On shore, the first sign of the wave was actually the water being sucked out to sea. Animals sensed danger and ran inland.

- The earthquake happened along a 1,000-mi. (1,600-km) length of the seabed.

- The Indian Ocean earthquake moved around 7.2 cubic mi. (30 cubic km) of sea water, which caused the tsunami.

HURRICANE KATRINA

August 23–30, 2005

Hurricane Katrina was the costliest natural disaster and the fifth deadliest in the history of the United States.

Hurricane Katrina first passed over Florida before heading toward Louisiana and Mississippi. Before making landfall, wind speeds reached 175 mph (282 kph) with gusts up to 215 mph (346 kph). The most damage was in New Orleans, where parts of the city are already below sea level. The hurricane's storm surge caused 53 levee (embankments) breaks. Around 80 percent of the city was left under water, and 60,000 people were stranded for days with no food or water.

Sunken City

In Mississippi and Alabama, storm waters reached up to 12 mi. (19 km) inland. Streets, bridges, and buildings were washed away.

The death toll for Katrina was 1,836 people, but many more were left homeless or unemployed. Also millions of acres (hectares) of forests were destroyed, and oil refineries in the Gulf of Mexico were shut down.

WHERE IN THE WORLD
New Orleans, Louisiana, as well as Mississippi, Alabama, and Florida.

USA

Mississippi · New Orleans

Florida

Atlantic Storm
Right: Helicopter patrols search for survivors. Below: The intensity and counterclockwise wind flow of the hurricane as seen from this satellite photo.

FACTS

• More than one million people were moved away from the Central Gold Coast and have not returned.

• After Hurricane Katrina, the designs of the levees were changed. The organization of the rescue was strongly criticized.

• Although people were warned that the hurricane was coming, not everyone in New Orleans was able, or wanted, to leave the city.

• Days after the hurricane passed, people died of thirst or exhaustion.

SICHUAN EARTHQUAKE

May 12, 2008

The nearer an earthquake is to the Earth's surface, the more the ground shakes. The Sichuan earthquake was only 11.8 mi. (19 km) deep.

Sichuan is a poorer, mountainous, mainly farming area in China. At 2.30 PM, a 7.9 earthquake hit with many strong aftershocks. Buildings slid down hillsides, crashing into one another, roads collapsed, and mudslides swept through towns.

Corruption

Mountains and heavy rains made rescue efforts more difficult. However, a lot of schools collapsed, killing 5,335 children. It became clear that school buildings had not been built according to safety laws.

More than 68,000 people and 12.5 million animals were killed in the earthquake and 5 million people were left homeless. About 12.5 million animals were killed.

WHERE IN THE WORLD
Sichuan province, western China. The epicenter was 50 mi. (80 km) west-northwest of Sichuan's capital Chengdu.

RUSSIA

Beijing

Sichuan Province

Chengdu • CHINA

INDIA

Building Collapse
Left: Rescue workers among the rubble. Below: The Chinese Army helps carry the wounded to hospitals and the dead to emergency mortuaries.

FACTS

• Months after the Sichuan earthquake, strong aftershocks were still being felt across China.

• In the town of Beichuan, 80 percent of the buildings collapsed in this earthquake.

• It was the strongest earthquake to hit China since 1950.

• This was the deadliest earthquake to hit China since the 1976 Tangshan earthquake, which killed more than 240,000 people.

HAITI EARTHQUAKE

Haiti is the poorest country in the western hemisphere. When an earthquake measuring 7.0 struck, the effect was catastrophic.

The epicenter of the earthquake was about 25 mi. (16 km) west of Haiti's capital, Port-au-Prince. The earthquake struck at 4.53 PM on a Tuesday, but within the next two weeks at least 52 aftershocks measuring at least 4.5 were recorded.

More than 250,000 homes were destroyed or severely damaged. Essential services, including the airport, seaport, telephone service, and hospitals, were seriously damaged. Roads were blocked, making it very difficult for rescue workers to reach the injured.

Homeless

It has been estimated that 300,000 people were injured and 316,000 people died in the quake and aftermath. With Port-au-Prince's morgues full, bodies had to be buried in mass graves. Many survivors were left homeless and slept in the streets.

WHERE IN THE WORLD
Haiti is in the western part of the island of Hispaniola in the Caribbean. It neighbors the Dominican Republic.

Rescue Work
Right: Survivors wander Haiti's ruined streets.
Below: A city of tents for survivors in Port-au-Prince eight months after the earthquake.

FACTS

• The prison in Port-au-Prince was also destroyed, allowing 4,000 inmates to escape.

• More than 1,300 schools were destroyed in the earthquake.

• At least three people drowned when a tsunami swept them out to sea.

• In October 2010, poor sanitation caused a cholera epidemic. By January 2013, it had killed more than 7,900 people.

TOHOKU EARTHQUAKE, TSUNAMI, AND MELTDOWN

WHERE IN THE WORLD

The epicenter of the earthquake was 43 mi. (70 km) east of Oshika Peninsula in Japan.

March 11, 2011

Disaster strikes when you combine a powerful earthquake, a devastating tsunami, and a nuclear meltdown.

The 9.0 magnitude earthquake happened under the sea and caused a tsunami. When the waves reached land, some of them were 133 ft. (40 m) high, and in some places they traveled 6 mi. (10 km) inland. Warning messages were sent out to millions of Japanese people, who headed for safer ground. However, this tsunami was bigger than expected. There were more than 15,000 deaths, and almost a million buildings were either destroyed or damaged.

Radiation Leak

As soon as the earthquake happened, the nuclear reactors at the Fukushima I Power Plant shut down. But the tsunami flooded the plant's generator rooms, cutting power to the pumps that kept the reactors cool. Without this water, the reactors began a nuclear meltdown, releasing toxic radiation. As far as 37 mi. (60 km) away, radiation levels were higher than safety limits allowed.

Poisoned Sea

Right: Buildings destroyed by the tsunami. Below: Workers in protective clothing are checked for radiation. Fukushima was the largest nuclear disaster since Chernobyl in 1986.

FACTS

- This was the most powerful earthquake known to have hit Japan.

- Sea water was used to cool the Fukushima nuclear reactors, but it washed back out to sea, spreading more radiation.

- Two nuclear reactor workers died as a result of the earthquake, but it is expected that up to 100 people will develop cancers caused by radiation.

- Possible radiation exposure caused a 12 mi. (20 km) zone to be evacuated.

HURRICANE SANDY

October 22–31, 2012

In October 2012, a large Atlantic hurricane formed in the Caribbean and headed for the eastern seaboard of North America.

Hurricane Sandy first hit Jamaica as a Category 1 storm. It pulled down power lines and left 70 percent of the population without electricity. From there it strengthened and passed over Haiti, Cuba, and the Bahamas.

Unusually warm water off the east coast of the U.S. helped the hurricane to develop further. A high pressure system over Greenland pushed Sandy back toward the east coast of the U.S. and Canada.

Evacuating the City

Sandy first made landfall in the U.S. at Atlantic City, New Jersey. The big waves flooded streets, snapped trees, and pulled down power lines, leaving almost two million people without electricity. In New York City, the Stock Exchange and the subway system were closed. When the hurricane hit, streets, roads, and car and subway tunnels were flooded.

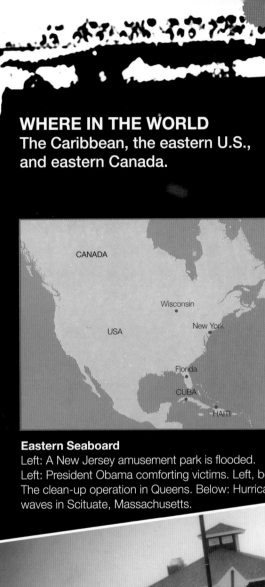

WHERE IN THE WORLD
The Caribbean, the eastern U.S., and eastern Canada.

Eastern Seaboard
Left: A New Jersey amusement park is flooded.
Left: President Obama comforting victims. Left, below: The clean-up operation in Queens. Below: Hurricane waves in Scituate, Massachusetts.

Frankenstorm Sandy

Frankenstorm Sandy's strength and angle of approach combined with a cold front coming in from the midwest to create a massive storm.

Hurricane Sandy affected 24 U.S. states, including the entire eastern seaboard from Florida to Maine. It reached as far west as Wisconsin, with the worst damage being done in New Jersey and New York State.

After the Storm
Above left: Cape May, New Jersey, pounded by waves.
Above: Hurricane Sandy caused severe flooding in Haiti. Left and far left: New York City was flooded.
Below: The destroyed rollercoaster at Seaside Heights, New Jersey.

FACTS

• Across seven countries, 253 people were killed by the hurricane.

• More than 7.9 million people were without power as temperatures dropped into the 20s F (-6 C) across the eastern seaboard.

• Winds from Hurricane Sandy spanned 1,100 mi. (1,800 km).

• The total amount of damage in the U.S. is estimated to have cost more than $63 billion.

INDEX